The Ten Truths For Raising a Healthy Bouncy Business

ROLAND HANEKROOT

© Copyright 2011 Roland Hanekroot – New Perspectives Coaching

All rights reserved.

No part of this publication may be reproduced or transmitted in any form or by any means, mechanical or electronic, including photocopying and recording, or by Information storage and retrieval systems, without permission in writing from Roland Hanekroot.

All material on the websites owned by Roland Hanekroot (including but not limited to www.newperspectives.com.au, www.thetentruths.com.au, www.smallbusinessbootcamp.com.au) is also subject to copyright. Request for further information can be directed to:

Roland Hanekroot
at New Perspectives Coaching
PO Box 1052 Potts Point 2011 NSW Australia

as well as admin@newperspectives.com.au.

Published by New Perspectives Publishing

Legal Notices

DISCLAIMER Whilst every effort has been made to ensure that the information contained within this book was obtained from reliable sources, the information was presented for general purposes only. The information is provided with the understanding that the author or the publisher are not rendering legal, professional or expert advice.

The author nor the publisher accept any responsibility for errors or omissions or for the results obtained from using the information. The application and impact of any information gained from this book can vary based on individual circumstances and the specific facts involved. All information in this book is provided without guarantee or warranty of any kind, express or implied.

In no event will Roland Hanekroot or the publisher accept any liability to anyone for any losses or damages that may arise as a result of a decision made or action taken in reliance upon the information contained in this book.

You are free to use any or all of the information in this book in support of making decisions or taking actions as you see fit while at the same time accepting full and complete responsibility for any consequences that may follow from those decisions and actions.

While every effort has been made to ensure that details and addresses of books, articles, videos and websites throughout this book are accurate at time of publication. No responsibility or liability is taken for the continued accuracy of these details. Also, the author and the publisher take no responsibility or liability for the content of these resources.

Cover and page design by Leah Klugt, The Golden Goose Design Studio
Illustrations by Kath Mayer

ISBN 978-0-9870794-8-0

Dedication

This book is dedicated to small business owners everywhere, thank you for inspiring me.

Contents

Introduction	**09**
Why this book?	10
What are *The Ten Truths* about?	12
The structure of this book	13
Where do *The Ten Truths* come from?	14
Acknowledgements	16
Feedback, questions, comments & support	18
Truth 1: About the Business Purpose	**21**
What is it all about?	22
John's Bedtime Story	25
Truth 2: About Planning	**29**
How is it going to get there?	30
Mel's Bedtime Story	34
Truth 3: About keeping your Finger on the Pulse	**41**
Are we actually getting there?	42
Georgie's Bedtime Story	46
Truth 4: About Financial Management	**51**
Are we making money?	52
Bob's Bedtime Story	55

Truth 5: About Marketing — 59
How do we create opportunities to do business? — 60
Josh's Bedtime Story — 64

Truth 6: About Customers — 69
Who are they, where are they, what do they need? — 70
Daniel's Bedtime Story — 73

Truth 7: About Sales — 77
How do we convert our 'stuff' to income? — 78
Kate's Bedtime Story — 81

Truth 8: About Operations — 85
How do we best produce our 'stuff'? — 86
Matt's Bedtime Story — 88

Truth 9: About Staff — 93
How do we engage our people? — 94
Tony's Bedtime Story — 96

Truth 10: About the Business Owner — 103
How do we get what we need from our business? — 104
Megan's Bedtime Story — 106

Bonus Truth — 111
About *The Small Business Bootcamp*™: — 111
How do we make it all happen? — 112

About the Author: — 118

INTRODUCTION

THE TEN TRUTHS

for Raising a Healthy Bouncy Business

Why this book?

The world is full of books, newsletters and websites that list the "Top 5 Tips to...", the "16 Rules for Selling Your..." or the "10 Things to Do Before...".

Why do we need another one?

Because this book is about timeless truths; ten of them. *The Ten Truths* are just that: absolutely true. I believe no one can or will argue them.

Some people may argue that there are 11 or 26 truths, others that the order in which I am going to present *The Ten Truths* to you is back to front, or upside down. But I am confident that no one will argue that *The Ten Truths for Raising a Healthy Bouncy Business* are false.

I know I might be accused of arrogance, making a statement like that - and I am ok with that. Some things are beyond argument. If I drop a glass out of my office window it will break when it hits the concrete six floors below. Similarly, if you implement *The Ten Truths* in your business consistently, being a small business owner will undoubtedly become a much more rewarding experience.

That in itself is a good enough reason to publish this book about *The Ten Truths*. I absolutely believe that if you own a small business, you will want to read about them.

The second reason why this book is needed, is that it includes a lot of resources and tools to assist you on your journey to raising your own Healthy Bouncy Business. Use them well. You won't regret it.

Finally, there is a third reason we need this book. Why I think you might want to read it if you are business owner, are married to one, the parent of one, you are thinking of becoming one, or if your work involves supporting one. And that is this:

You will have noticed that the title of this book is a play on words. 'Raising a healthy bouncy baby' is a common expression. I have replaced the word 'baby' with 'business', because I want you to think of creating and developing a business as a truly creative act. It is the second most creative thing any of us human beings can do in life, after creating and raising a baby.

A business owner develops an idea in his head, creates this idea in the real world and then breathes life into it. Once the business is alive, we have the 'Terrible Twos', 'Teething Troubles', 'Growing Pains', 'Sleepless Nights', 'Adolescence' – and finally we have to let the business go to stand on its own two legs (although we probably still end up doing the laundry for it every Sunday for a year or two).

Most business owners I have worked with tell me at some point that they aren't very creative. They say they leave creativity to the 'creative types'. The deeper purpose (see chapter 1, Truth 1) of this book and the work I do with *The Ten Truths* and in *The Small Business Bootcamp*™ (see chapter 11) is to change the way small business owners think of themselves, and how our society sees them. Just like great artists, small business owners are passionate, excited, driven – and they take enormous risks and let their imagination roam to create expressions of themselves.

The third reason for writing this book therefore is to encourage small business owners to let their creativity roam free.

What are The Ten Truths about?

There are ten aspects common to every business:

These are:

1. Mission and Purpose: What is the business about and where is it heading?

2. Planning: How is it going to get to where it is headed?

3. Control and Measurement: How can we tell if we are heading in the right direction?

4. Financial Management: Are we making money?

5. Marketing: How do we create opportunities to do business?

6. Customers: Who are they, where are they, what do they want from us?

7. Sales: How do we convert our communications into income?

8. Operations: How do we produce the stuff our customers want from us?

9. Staff: How do we relate to the people in our business?

10. The Business Owner: How do we look after ourselves and get what we want from our business?

Every business is affected by these ten aspects in one way or another. And every business owner needs to remind himself of the related questions on a regular basis.

When you have a Healthy Bouncy Business, you will be able to answer these questions with *The Ten Truths*.

I refer to the first three Truths as the *Primary Truths*. This is because these three Truths stand like an umbrella over the remaining seven. You must have a solid understanding of these three to be able to make headway with all the rest, the *Secondary Truths*. The chart at the end of this introduction shows how it all hangs together.

The last chapter (number 11) reveals what I refer to as a *Bonus Truth*, because it isn't a truth about small business so much as a truth about execution and implementation. How are you actually going to make a Healthy Bouncy Business happen - every day?

The structure of this book

There is a chapter for each of *The Ten Truths*. Each chapter begins with a concise explanation of the Truth, and a mind map or a graphic illustrating the important concepts and connections.

Following the explanation of each Truth there is a little story about one of my clients' experiences of this Truth in their business. The stories describe real people and real situations, but the identities have been altered.

Then there will be a short series of next steps. These will

be some simple actions that you as a small business owner can start to take today, to begin the process of aligning your business with *The Ten Truths*.

At the end of each Truth chapter is a list of resources such as books, blogs or articles to delve deeper into one or more of the Truths. There will also be updated and new resources on the www.thetentruths.com.au website.

Throughout you will find illustrations of our budding entrepreneur Little Richard (no relation to either singer or mega entrepreneur), to show us how it's done.

The final chapter *Bonus Truth*, talks about how to actually go about making all this good stuff happen in your business.

Read the Truths. Do a bit of further reading via the resources if your interest in the Truths is engaged. Heed the lessons of the last chapter about getting in to action. Implement the next steps one by one. And you will find that being the parent of a Healthy Bouncy Business is one of the most challenging, exciting and rewarding journeys you will experience in your life.

Where do *The Ten Truths* come from?

Not much of what follows is entirely new or groundbreaking. New ideas are few and far between in life. Socrates, Newton and Einstein might have had a few of totally new ideas between them. But when Einstein was once asked how it was possible for him to have developed all of his great theories, his answer was: "Because I stand on the shoulders of giants". And Socrates' ideas did not lead to a happy end in ancient Greece either. Too many people lay claim to 'original IP' for my liking. Most of what I have done in this book is to combine ideas and insights from many different sources and authors, and added my own spin and emphasis. Some of the authors and thinkers are referred to in the resources sections of each chapter.

This book is also not a scientific book. I like to think of *The Ten Truths* as time honoured or timeless, as I mentioned above. What I can say, categorically, is that I have observed them to be true many times over.

So this is where I found *The Ten Truths*:

1. My clients: I work with and support small business owners to raise Healthy Bouncy Businesses and have done so for nearly seven years. I am constantly blown away with how much I learn from my clients, and some of my insights that are reflected in *The Ten Truths* come directly from my clients.

2. My own businesses: Prior to becoming what I am now, I created and raised several small businesses, starting in the early eighties. Some of these businesses were very healthy and bouncy, some less so. You can be sure that I learnt valuable lessons from those 25 years, and some of them have found their way into *The Ten Truths*.

3. Book stores: Also, in the past ten years, a lot of my life has been about study on many fronts; business management not least amongst them. I believe I have become a favourite customer of a number of bookstores, and in spite of the state of

my ageing addled brain, I did pick up a few useful insights from weighty tomes. Some of which have definitely found their way into *The Ten Truths*.

4. Other coaches: Finally, in the last three years I have worked intensively with a group of small business coaches to develop a new business coaching methodology. The work we did over a period of two years led to my unique coaching program called *The Small Business Bootcamp*™ (see the last chapter of this book and my website www.newperspectives.com.au. Working with the group, especially Lesley Schoer from Coffs Harbour in NSW has been enormously stimulating and rich in learning. *The Ten Truths* were born as a concept in my head while working with this group of people.

Acknowledgements

This book has been growing in my head for the past three years. A number of people have been instrumental in its gestation a special thank you to all of them:

- **Lesley Schoer** www.lesleyschoer.com.au has been a great source of inspiration, solid advice and input in the project.

- **Merryl Naughton** www.howtogetapayrise.com showed me that all you need to do to get a book project going, is just to decide to do it and not make a big fuss about it.

- **Rebecca Wells** www.askrebeccahow.com has been a wonderful coach, support and friend in the past year.
- **Amanda Crawford** www.periplum.com.au/ has been my brilliant editor.

And finally, all my clients who I learn from, who challenge and inspire me every day, and whom I can never get enough of. I could fill two pages with the names of clients I have learnt something powerful from; here are just a few:

- **David Jones,** David Jones Electricians: *"You are in Safe Hands"* www.djelectricians.com.au
- **Simon Wahid**, 7 Star Supermarkets: *"The Best Small Supermarket in Sydney"* www.7starsupermarket.com.au
- **Mathew Stubbs**, MS Partners *"Architecture that Inspires"* www.mspartners.com.au
- **Stella Gianotto**, Stella Design: *"Because There is No Excuse for Bad Design"* www.stelladesign.com.au
- **Geoff Anderson**, Sonic Sight: *"It is a Joy to Work with Us"* www.sonicsight.com.au
- **Lawrence Hugh**, Collideascope: *"Cradle to the Grave Motorcycle Pampering"* www.collideascope.com.au

Last but not least I want to thank of course my proofreader, challenge, inspiration - oh, and gorgeous wife! - Daniela Cavalletti www.cavallletticommunications.com.au for being all of that.

Feedback, questions, comments & support

I would like to talk to you, to explore if *The Small Business Bootcamp* is what you need to get yourself and your business going. I would also love to hear your feedback on *The Ten Truths* and this book. I will be more than happy to answer any question you have about the tools or resources throughout this book.

I would especially like to hear your success stories about implementing any of *The Ten Truths*.

Simply drop me an email to roland@thetentruths.com.au or head to the website www.thetentruths.com.au. If you would like to know more about me, my philosophies and my coaching styles, please go to the New Perspectives website www.newperspectives.com.au. The main coaching, mentoring and small business consulting program I run is called The *Small Business Bootcamp*™. You can read about how it works and what you will get out of at www.smallbusinessbootcamp.com.au.

I promise to respond usefully to every genuine email and promptly. If you don't agree with anything I have written, I look forward to discussing it with you.

From time to time I will make more resources and tools available through the *The Ten Truths* website, and under the *The Ten Truths*-brand. Send me an email with your details, if you want me to keep you in the loop.

A note about the text: I have decided to refer to business owners in this book as male (he, him, his). I could just as easily have chose to make the business owners females. As a matter of fact more than half my clients have been women. I believe more and more women start and raise very successful small businesses as it becomes clear that being the owner of a business is a pretty effective way to avoid the glass ceiling.

Of course any errors are mine and mine alone.

This is only the beginning. I have ordered millions of plastic *The Ten Truths* Babies, as well as stickers, building blocks, magnets, notepads, and all kinds of merchandising. And I am in discussions with McDonald's to create the *The Ten Truths Burger*. Coming to a store near you very soon...

Enjoy and experiment with the concepts in this book, play with them. As the American Business Guru Jack Stack says: "Play the great game of business!"

Above all... Have fun with it.

The Ten Truths for Raising a Healthy Bouncy Business

1. Vision/Purpose
What is the business about and where is it headed?
Truth 1:
A Business Without True Purpose and Passion... isn't

2. Planning
How is it going to get where it is headed?
Truth 2:
A Business Without a Plan Achieves everything in it

3. Control and Measurement
Can we tell if it is heading in the right direction?
Truth 3:
Gaze into the future, with your Finger firmly on the Pulse, Weekly

The Primary Truths

4. Financial management
Are we making money?
Truth 4:
A Healthy Bouncy Business makes turnover, cash and profit

5. Marketing
How do we create opportunities to do business?
Truth 5:
Marketing is everything, and everything is marketing

6. Customers
Who are they, where are they, what do they want from us?
Truth 6:
Create Raving Fans; Satisfied Customers aren't Good Enough anymore

7. Sales
How do we convert out communications into income?
Truth 7:
Nothing Happens until we Sell Something

The Secondary Truths

8. Operations
How do we produce the stuff our customers want from us?
Truth 8:
Do More of what Works and Less of what Doesn't Work

9. People
How do we relate to all of "Our People"?
Truth 9:
Attract the Brightest; Keep the Brightest

10. The Owner
How do we look after ourselves and get what we want from our business?
Truth 10:
Your Time and your Health are The Gold in your Business

TRUTH 1
About the Business Purpose

A business without true purpose and passion… isn't

What is it all about?

> *If you don't care about the 'why' of your business, no one else will either.*

The first of the three primary Truths is that the owner of a Healthy Bouncy Business must be clear about its purpose and its future. The questions: "Why does your business exist on this earth?" or "What is so special about your business?" must have instant, clear and unambiguous answers. Most importantly, the answers must be based on the personal values and passions of the owner(s).

Only once the owner is absolutely clear why he is in this business - what it is all about for him, why it excites and inspires him - will he be able to create a powerful business 'Mission and Purpose' that will enthuse his staff, his customers and everyone connected with the business.

> **The Mission and Purpose sits behind every part, every action, every decision of the business. It informs how all the other parts of the business operate.**

We define the business Mission and Purpose in a statement that clarifies what the whole of the business strives for. It is an inspiring visionary statement that excites, and drives everyone who is part of the business. It fulfils a common need for people, which is to be part of something bigger.

One example of a great business Mission and Purpose statement comes from a furniture manufacturer in Sydney, Nicholas Dattner. Nicholas created a work shop and retail outlet in the mid-eighties in Sydney, selling tables and chairs that he made himself. He named the business:

'The World's Most Beautiful Tables'

Nicholas Dattner's business became very successful and many fine homes in Sydney have one of his tables in their dining room. Nicholas himself is sailing around the world these days and will not need to work anymore for the rest of his life.

The impact of such a single courageous statement is to give a clarity, direction and focus to the business that makes every decision and action in the business so much easier to take.

Once you have developed a clear, inspiring, unambiguous Mission and Purpose, an important next step is to create a set of Guiding Principles, or Commandments which define the behaviours and decisions that lead to achievement of the Mission and Purpose. Without such a set of Guiding Principles, it is likely that the mission will get watered down and loses its impact over time.

With a Mission and Purpose, and Guiding Principles, in place the business will really be able to engage and motivate its people by means other than money.

How do your personal values relate to what your business does?

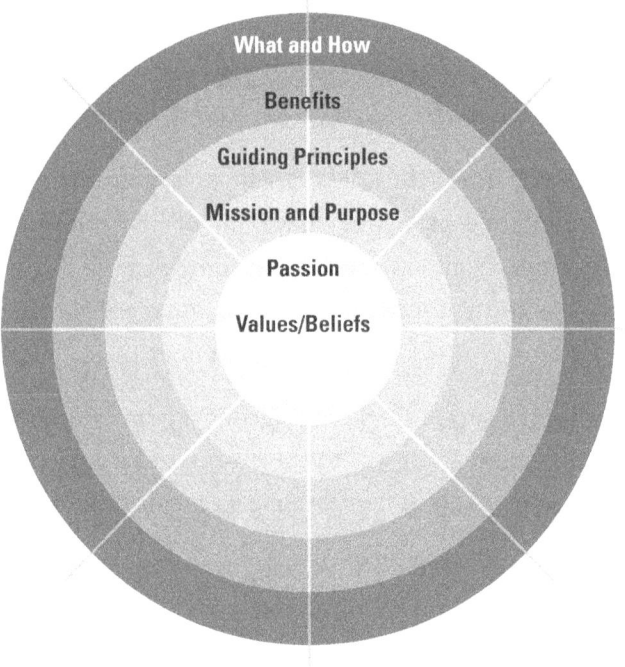

It all starts with your personal values and beliefs. They drive what you are passionate about, which in turn leads to your Mission, Cause or Purpose. The Guiding Principles flow from that, leading to the benefits we want to provide the customers with. And the last step is to decide how we are going to achieve that.

John's Bedtime Story

Once upon a time a long, long time ago in a land not unlike Australia... I worked with a small business owner called John, who had an electrical contracting business. John felt that his business had been drifting aimlessly from job to job for some time. Staff were not particularly engaged with the business.

One day John and I realised that because John himself wasn't particularly clear on what the business was about or why it existed, he could hardly ask anyone else to be engaged with it.

Over a period of some weeks, we went through a process to unearth what John himself was really all about, why he did what he did, and hence what the purpose of his company was. In the end, we honed in on the connection between John's passion and why the business existed. We expressed this in one short statement: "You're in Safe Hands"

Suddenly things started to fall into place. The whole direction and focus of the business became clear. John was able to communicate this to his staff and engage them in it. He knew he was on the right track with his mission when some of his staff started pointing out systems and procedures in the business that were at odds with the purpose of "You're in safe Hands".

Now, a few years later, it's hard to recognise the business. The brand and the purpose have become one and everyone associated with the company lives the purpose every day.

And John lived happily ever after...

Next Steps

1. Ask other successful business owners what their purpose was when they started their business.

2. Download the Passion and Purpose worksheet from the resources section and work through the steps. This worksheet asks all the questions to help you identify your mission and purpose.

3. Write down your organisation's purpose: clear, unique and credible.

4. Share your thoughts on sense of purpose with others, ask for feedback.

5. Use a voice recorder and listen to yourself tell the company's founding story. Be sure it is interesting, indicative of what the company is really all about and conveys an overall moral lesson.

Resources

- *The Ten Truths* Website: www.thetentruths.com.au/resources/purpose
- Book – Jason Jennings, "It is Not the Big that Eat the Small, it is the Fast that Eat the Slow" www.amazon.com/Its-That-Small-Its-Fast-Slow/dp/0066620546/ref=sr_1_1?ie=UTF8&s=books&qid=1286766869&sr=1-1
- Book – by Steven Little, "The 7 Irrefutable Rules for Small Business Growth" www.amazon.com/Irrefutable-Rules-Small-Business-Growth/dp/0471707600/ref=pd_bxgy_b_img_a
- Video – Simon Sinek, "People don't buy what you do, they buy why you do it": www.youtube.com/watch?v=u4ZoJKF_VuA&feature=player_embedded
- Worksheet – Passion and Purpose: www.thetentruths.com.au/Downloads/Passion_and_purpose_worksheet.pdf

Remember

When you are absolutely crystal clear why your business is on this earth, what it exists for, everything else suddenly becomes clear.

TRUTH 2

About the Planning

A business without a plan achieves everything in it

How is it going to get there?

Napoleon: No battle plan ever survives the first contact with the enemy.

The two statements above about planning seem to be contradictory. Yet both statements are true if you think about business planning not as the completed document, but the process of planning. What Truth 2 tells us is, that it is the work, the thinking and the time that is invested in developing the Plans that is essential to create a Healthy Bouncy Business. That is why Truth 2 is the second of the Primary Truths.

Planning creates the roadmap for a business: where it is going, what it will achieve, how and when it will achieve these things, and what you - the business owner - wants to get out of it.

> **Planning needs time and considered thought. It requires that you step back from the day-to-day detail of working <u>in</u> the business to think, analyse, make decisions, monitor and plan changes - in other words, to work <u>on</u> the business.**

In planning for a Healthy Bouncy Business, decisions must be made about the strategies that you will use to get the business where you want it to be. In order to make these decisions you need to know what's going on in and around the business, and what is likely to impact the business - now and in the future.

One of the first steps to business planning involves analysing where the business is now, deciding where you want it to go and thinking about what the opportunities and hurdles are for it to get there. A classic tool to do this with is a SWOT analysis in which the Strengths, Weaknesses, Opportunities and Threats to and of the business are identified and analysed. A thorough SWOT analysis will also include consideration of the external environment in which the business operates. The economic, environmental, social and cultural factors that influence the business and its success. Although most of these external factors are outside of your control, planning your response to possible changes and developments in these external areas will allow you to be pro-active in your business decisions and activities rather than re-active.

A culture of pro-active decision making in a business is one of the greatest indicators for long term sustainable success.

There are no generally accepted definitions of what a business plan should look like, what it must include and what form it must be in. There are many different appearances a business plan can take, but the planning process usually results in some type of written or visual document setting out the goals, analyses and strategies for the business.

The first step in the planning process is to decide who the plan is for, and what the intended use of the plan is.

There are two distinctively different types of business plan: an external plan and an internal plan. An external plan is created to make a business case to a third party - such as a bank as part of a loan application or an investor to make a capital injection. An internal business plan is created to drive strategy, focus and actions inside the business. It is the ultimate tool that is used throughout the business to set directions with, and to frame decisions.

The type of planning process you go through, and the plan that results, depends on how you will use it. An external plan will nearly always be created in a formal standardised structure, whereas an internal plan can take any form from a single page document to a whole ring binder with many different sections appropriate to all parts of the business.

The fact is that most business owners have avoided creating a business plan because they have an image of a formal business plan of many pages with 'executive summaries' and 'market analyses' and 'PEST' studies etc. That image is overwhelming, and so they just put it in the 'too hard basket'. In the meantime they allow their internal critic to remind them at regular intervals that they 'should' start writing that business plan.

Planning doesn't have to be daunting, though. What matters, is that you end up with a tool that helps you drive the business forward. In whatever shape works best for you.

The most extreme example of a 'Very Short and Very Useful Business Plan' is that of a friend of mine. Paul owns a successful painting and decorating company. His plan is the simplest I have come across. It is one page and it has three statements on it:

1. Local
2. By the book
3. Charge enough to do a good job

These three statements frame his direction and focus and give context to all decisions in the business, every day.

'Planning is guessing'

Planning to raise a Healthy Bouncy Business is not about writing a document that is set in concrete. It is a big mistake to think of a plan as a finished, polished document that determines what the future is going to look like. We can't actually know what tomorrow will bring. At best, the plan will be an educated guess of what the future may be. Effective planning is therefore a continual process of keeping informed with internal and external issues. Ensuring the business is prepared, equipped and capable of taking up opportunities and managing threats in the future.

A business plan that works is a 'living' document, a copy of which is visible on every desk in the business. It has coffee stains all over it and notes scribbled in the margin. There is a process in the business for updating and reviewing the plan which all stakeholders in the business are involved in, as a minimum on a yearly basis.

A 'living' plan helps the business stay true to its Mission and Purpose (see Truth 1), while achieving what you want for it. With a 'living' plan, you have a tool for ensuring you raise a Healthy Bouncy Business.

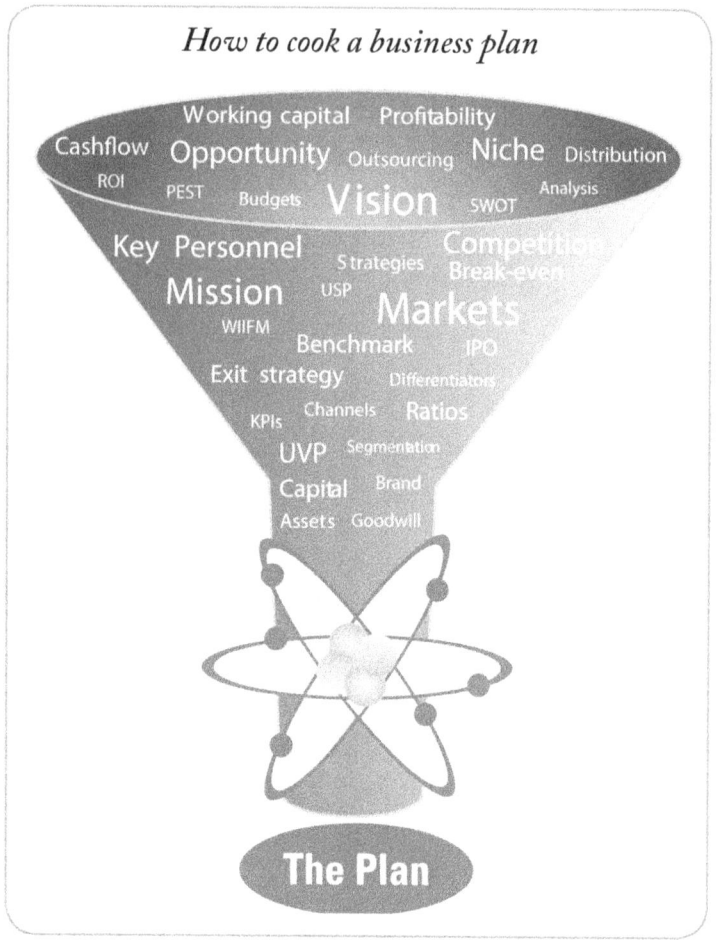

Mel's Bedtime Story

Once upon a time a long, long time ago in a land not unlike Australia... I worked with a small business owner called Mel, who owned a management and IT consulting firm. While working with me, Mel spent months creating her business plan for the next three years. Part of the planning process involved building an organisational chart around her existing employees and the kinds of people she expected to employ in the foreseeable future. Given that Mel was a management consultant herself, she was very familiar with creating such charts. The result was impressive and looked perfectly suited for the future.

However, in the week after she completed her organisational chart an old friend and colleague of hers with a much smaller but similar business rang, and told her he was looking for a job. He no longer wanted his own practice and wanted to come on board with Mel in a senior capacity. And he was offering to merge his business into hers for a very reasonable price. The opportunity was very exciting and, handled correctly, would open up enormous potential for Mel's business.

Obviously Mel's business plan didn't and couldn't have foreseen anything like this. The brand new organisation chart instantly became so much scrap paper. However, because Mel had spent the time planning and really coming to grips with the different roles, responsibilities and deliverables within her organisation, she was able to quickly shuffle things around and sketch out a new chart with the proverbial 3B pencil on the back of her old chart. One conversation and 24 hours later Mel accepted her friend's offer. A month later the new structure was in place and humming.

Even though the original plan turned out to be fantasy, the process of planning and the attention Mel had given to the process allowed her to make quick and accurate decisions and move forward confidently.

And Mel lived happily ever after...

Next Steps

As I mentioned above, a plan can be a single page document with a couple of critical statements on it, or it can be as big as a full ring binder.

The first step therefore is to decide what a truly useful plan would look like for your business. If you decide to create a plan that includes documentation about all the facets of the business - for all *Ten Truths* areas if you will - then this could be a good way to go about it:

1. Buy a new loose leaf binder and label it 'Business Plan' or 'Growth Plan' or 'My Business Future' or 'Directions' or something meaningful to you.

2. Collect all documentation of your business (in whatever form you have it), such as scripts for telephone answering, or lists of advertising and marketing channels. Procedures for changing the toner in the copier, financial budgets, old proposals to financial institutions for loan applications. Include checklists for order receipt or dispatch; for quoting or proposal writing. Add copies of standard quote and invoice forms, templates for letters of demand, team strategy documents.

3. Don't forget IT procedures, such as backing up or virus protection. Collect your marketing brochures and style guides from the designer who created your stationary. Add samples of your stationary, resources spreadsheets, scheduling documentation, etc.
   Include any tool you use to run the business.

4. Decide what kind and form of plan would be useful for your business at this stage.

5. Create a content page for your 'Business Plan' and put it in the folder. The content page might have headings in line with *The Ten Truths* aspects of Business Purpose, Planning, Control, Financial Management, etc.

6. Sort whatever documentation you have collected already into the appropriate section in the folder.

7. Create a list of the obvious gaps in the folder. You might find that you have lots of stuff in the 'Marketing' section but virtually nothing in the 'Sales' section, for example.

8. Decide where to go from here, create a plan and timeline for the project (a realistic one).

9. Start somewhere. It really doesn't matter... Pick the big thing first or pick 'the low hanging fruit' - just start somewhere.

10. Ask someone you trust: to work with you on it and keep you accountable to the project plan and timeline.

Resources

- *The Ten Truths* Website: www.thetentruths.com.au/resources/planning
- Article – Business Planning Step by Step, from the NSW Government www.thetentruths.com.au/Downloads/BusinessPlanning_basics_NSW_gov.pdf
- Book – Jason Fried and David Heinemeier Hansson,: "Rework" www.amazon.com/Rework-Jason-Fried/dp/0307463745
- Worksheet – Business Plan Template, from the Tasmanian Government www.thetentruths.com.au/Downloads/businessplan_tas_gov.dot
- Worksheet – Extended SWOT Analysis: www.thetentruths.com.au/Downloads/SWOT-extended.pdf

Remember

Planning is about the work we do to create the plan, not about the actual document.

TRUTH 3

About keeping your Finger on the Pulse

Gaze into the future with your finger firmly on the pulse - weekly

Are we actually getting there?

I have a magic coin that tells the future 50% of the time.

Being able to forecast the future with an accuracy greater than flipping a coin is the holy grail of entrepreneurship.

There is only one way to learn to make predictions about what will happen tomorrow, next week or next month: and that is to start with the past. Recording what happens in the business and doing so over time is therefore the third part of the nucleus of a Healthy Bouncy Business. A business owner must implement a system to check on the health of the business constantly, and to record the performance of the business across a range of key indicators - both short and long term.

Only by building up such systems and records will the business owner know where to focus his attention. They enable him to build up knowledge and insights that will allow him to make ever more accurate forecasts about workload, cash flow, profitability, staff needs, stock levels, marketing budgets, and other indicators, well into the future.

We could liken such a system to the dashboard of a car. A gauge for reading oil pressure, one for fuel level, and another one for temperature. They all tell the driver instantly if the car is travelling ok. If one of the needles moves out of a certain range, the driver can take immediate corrective action, such as pulling into a service station when the petrol gauge drops too low.

Besides the actual current data in the dashboard we also need a printout accumulating the data for the previous weeks and months, allowing the business owner to see trends and make predictions for the future.

A business Dashboard is a vital tool for the owner of a Healthy Bouncy Business because it allows him to focus on the important business building and entrepreneurial functions that only he can carry out.

> **With a well-designed Dashboard, the owner can delegate all the technical, administrative and operational roles within the business, while keeping his finger on the pulse of the various aspects of the business.**

A typical Dashboard of a small business might include weekly financial indicators for collections, payments made, work in progress, bank balance, accounts receivable, accounts payable, other current debt (GST, for example), and revenue as well as net profit for the year to date. For marketing there could be indicators for number of phone enquiries received, or the number of quotes sent out. There might be some indicators for customer satisfaction that week, or for staff motivation and engagement. There could be a ratio for staff utilisation, or billable hours. Or there might be an indicator that gives the business owner a handle on material wastage. The list of potential indicators is endless and will be different for every business and every business owner.

Relative, unscientific and approximate numbers

There is a secret tip I will share here about designing effective Dashboards in a business. People are often puzzled about how to measure anything in their business other than money. The secret is to give up the need to be absolutely accurate and scientific. What we need in a Dashboard is to be able to see if today was better than yesterday, or if we performed better or worse in a particular area of the business than last week. 99 times out of 100 you can walk up to a staff member on your factory floor or in the office, and they will be able to tell you whether the business ran smoother this week than last week; if the output was higher or more efficient than last week; if customers were happier or less happy than last week. People are very easily able to give themselves a score out of 10 for their own performance this week, and can do the same again next week and make a relative comparison. It is this relative comparison that we want to see. Did we do better this week or not? And how can we make sure that we do a little better again next week? As accountants often say: "The trend is my friend".

For example, I had a client who ran a restaurant. One of the indicators of the health of his business was to know how enticing each dish looked. Presentation is an enormous factor in client satisfaction in a restaurant. He agonised over finding a measurement for presentation. In the end he simply asked his head chef to give the kitchen a score for presentation every night out of 10: How good did our dishes look tonight out of 10? This was obviously far from a scientific method, but it gave him a simple set of seven figures to talk about with the head chef at his weekly operations meeting.

Without a cleverly designed Dashboard system, the business owner can do no more than flip his magic coin, hope that his staff are doing the right thing - and keep his fingers crossed in the mean time. The alternative is that he will spend so much time managing and supervising that the true work of the business owner - working on the business - gets neglected.

With a Dashboard in place the business owner of a Healthy Bouncy Business can make decisions about hiring staff, making investments, or other business factors confident of the future.

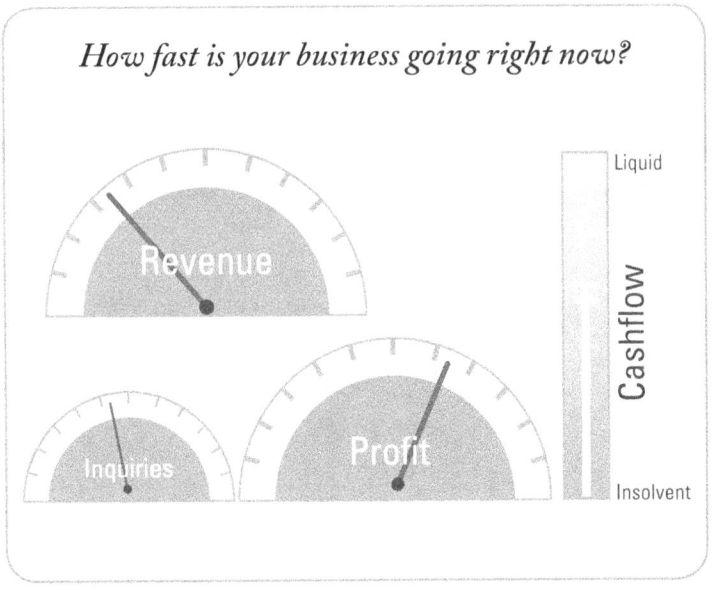

Georgie's Bedtime Story

Once upon a time a long, long time ago in a land not unlike Australia... I worked with a small business owner called Georgie, who was pregnant. Prior to her pregnancy Georgie worked an average 60 to 70 hours per week. Despite this, she never felt she really knew what was going on, but was always managing one crisis after another.

During her pregnancy she developed and implemented a Dashboard structure for three areas of her business: finances, production and sales. She made one staff member in each of these areas responsible for populating the Dashboard by Friday lunchtime every week.

Now that Georgie has had her baby, she comes to the office at 1 pm every Friday. In an one hour meeting with the three people responsible for their respective parts of the Dashboard, Georgie finds out exactly what is going well and what needs extra attention the following week. Besides the odd phone call about client matters, Georgie can focus on enjoying the time with her new baby.

And Georgie (and her baby) lived happily ever after...

Next Steps

1. Imagine that you have been banished to a beautiful desert island somewhere in the Pacific. The only connection with the rest of the world is the weekly mail boat, which brings you one piece of paper each week from your business with 15 (or 12, or 20) numbers on it. Those 15 numbers are the only source of information about the state of health of your business that you receive from week to week. What could those numbers be? What 15 numbers will tell you exactly how healthy your business is at that moment?

2. In other words, what must you absolutely know about your business each week?

3. Next, write down five things you would like to be able to forecast, one week out, one month out, and three months out.

4. Now you have 15 numbers about your business and 5 things you'd like to be able to forecast.

5. What sources are there for these 20 indicators (15+5)?

6. Who can get these numbers for you in your business, every week, and post them with the mail boat?

Resources

- *The Ten Truths* Website:
  www.thetentruths.com.au/resources/finger-on-the-pulse
- Article – Balanced Score Card Institute:
  www.balancedscorecard.org/BSCResources/AbouttheBalancedScorecard/tabid/55/Default.aspx
- Article – Stacey Barr on Dashboards:
  www.flyingsolo.com.au/working-smarter/productivity/business-dashboard-checklist
- Article – Valerie Khoo on Dashboards:
  www.blogs.theage.com.au/small-business/enterprise/2010/03/10/whyyourbusine.html
- Article – Wikipedia, on balanced score cards:
  www.en.wikipedia.org/wiki/Balanced_scorecard
- Worksheet – Simple dashboard example:
  www.thetentruths.com.au/Downloads/Ten-Truths-Dashboard.pdf

Remember

For the Dashboard report to be an effective business management tool, the business owner must delegate the preparation of the dashboard to his staff.

If the business owner prepares the dashboard himself a large part of the purpose of the weekly exercise is defeated.

Also, the Dashboard should include the least possible number of indicators of the health of the business. Less is more.

TRUTH 4
About Financial Management

A Healthy Bouncy Business makes turnover, cash and profit

Are we making money?

*Cash, profit and turnover have
nothing to do with each other*

A major cause of downfall of many small businesses is confusion between cash, profit and turnover in a business.

The state of the business' bank account is never an indication of the profitability of the business. And a business that is profitable may still not be able to pay its debts, can become insolvent and go out of business. Many service businesses especially have run aground while being incredibly busy - so busy that they neglect to invoice.

A business must carry out enough business turnover in a sufficiently profitable manner to pay for its overheads. It must bill profitably for that business regularly -weekly or even daily. And a business must collect payment for those bills as soon as possible, so it has enough cash in its bank account to meet its obligations when they are due. In most businesses there is virtually no direct connection between the three elements of turnover, profit and cash.

A plumbing business, for example, might complete one job on Tuesday that takes an hour. The business might be able to invoice the client $200 for the job and the raw cost to the business of this hour's work is only $50. This looks like a very healthy 300% profit margin.

However, until the day that the $200 is actually in the business' bank account as cleared funds, the business has a negative cash flow and needs to pay its costs from other funds. Moreover, as the cost to the business for one hour was $50, the business would have at least eight times that cost (i.e. for an 8hr work-day), or a total of $400 for a whole day of operation. The business must therefore send at least two of those invoices on a given day just to survive, or break even.

> **In a plumbing business it is expected to pay employees every Friday. And hence, unless the business actually collects that $400 by Friday as cleared funds, the employees have to be paid out of thin air.**

Turnover can be measured indirectly through job sheets or time sheets in a service business, or through indirect recording systems in manufacturing environments, for example.

Profit is measured in the 'Profit and Loss' reports that can be produced by a bookkeeping system. Profit is a function of the price that the business charges for its products or services, minus its direct and indirect expenses.

Cash directly impacts the business' ability to carry out its core functions. Profit impacts the long term survival of the business.

Cash is primarily reported via bank statements, and needs slightly more complicated systems to forecast and manage within bookkeeping systems. How much cash a business has in its accounts is directly related to payment and trading terms, and how rigorously they are adhered to in the business.

Many businesses become insolvent even though they showed good profitability, and just as many businesses have failed from 'living beyond their means' - simply because the bank account looked so flush.

In a Healthy Bouncing Business, equal attention is paid by the business owner to turnover, profitability and cash.

A simple mantra that the owner of a Healthy Bouncy Business repeats, over and over:

- I need to turnover $xxx per week
- I need to invoice $xxx per week
- I need to collect $xxx per week

Where $xxx is the respective minimum amount required to be profitable.

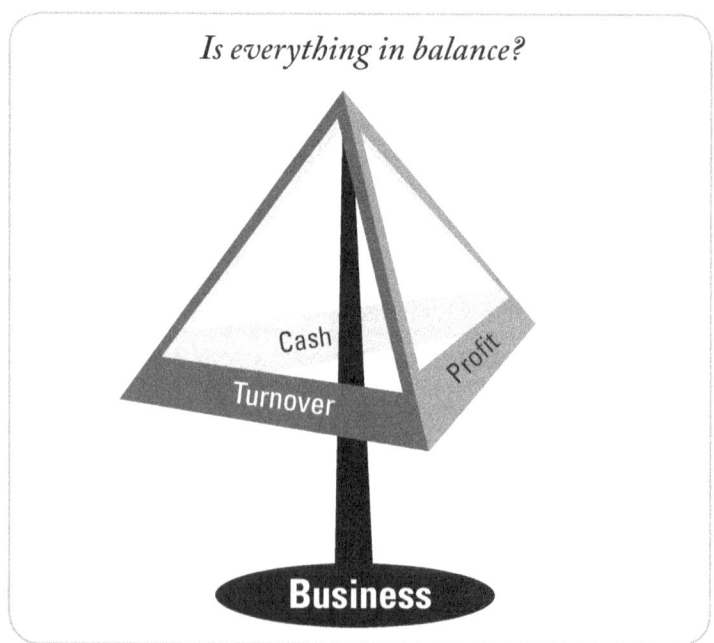

Bob's Bedtime Story

Once upon a time a long, long time ago in a land not unlike Australia... I worked with a small business owner called Bob, who had a solid plumbing business. When I started working with Bob he struggled every week to pay his bills, and many weeks he had to forgo his own wages to pay his boys. Bob and I worked out that he needed to deposit at least $6,500 in his bank account, 52 weeks of the year, to pay his bills. Allowing for holidays and Christmas - and including an allowance for profit -, Bob made it his mantra to carry out $8,000 worth of work, to invoice $8,000 and to collect $8,000, week in week out, 48 weeks of the year.

Within a month we started noticing a difference in his bank account, and it soon became obvious to Bob that clients who don't pay on time are not worth having. Bob started to become much choosier who he worked for. He actually 'fired' about 15% of his client base over the subsequent four months. At the end of our six month engagement, Bob's business had become the very essence of a Healthy Bouncy Business.

And Bob lived happily ever after...

Next Steps

1. Calculate what it costs you to open the doors each week.

2. Work out, or ask your accountant, what you have to charge/earn every week to break even.

3. How many days does it take you to collect payment, on average?

4. If you are growing, do you know what cash needs you will have?

5. Ask your accountant and/or business coach to help you set up some way to manage cash flow forecasting for your business.

Resources

- *The Ten Truths* Website: www.thetentruths.com.au/resources/finance
- Article – Roland Hanekroot: "Profits are a Liability" www.thetentruths.com.au/Downloads/Profits-are-a-liability.pdf
- Worksheet – Basic Cash flow forecasting, ANZ Bank: www.thetentruths.com.au/Downloads/Cash-Flow-Template-ANZ.xls
- Book & Website – Phillip CVampbell: "Never Run out of Cash" www.neverrunoutofcash.com

Remember

A business that does not make profit is a hobby.

And unless the profit actually hits your bank account you're better off going fishing.

TRUTH 5

About Marketing

Marketing is everything, and everything is marketing

How do we create opportunities to do business?

The most effective marketing strategy ever is called 'Talking to your Customers'.

Many business owners live under the mistaken impression that marketing consists of placing an advertisement in the Yellow Pages and waiting for the phone to ring.

This is certainly no longer true (if ever it was).

Sometimes it can be useful to substitute the terms 'lead generation', or 'creating opportunities to do business' for the word 'marketing', to help better understand what it is all about.

The best way to think about marketing is as a constant focus on building long term, productive and meaningful relationships with your existing and prospective customers.

A critical component of any marketing strategy is identification of what sets your business uniquely apart from any other business in the world. Why would anyone buy from you, as opposed to anyone else? If you can answer that question succinctly, and you have absolute clarity on the first Truth - the passion, purpose and 'why' of your business - your marketing strategies will fall into place.

> **Marketing a business, and its products or services, is both an art and a science. In a Healthy Bouncy Business, the business owner takes a medium to long term approach to marketing strategy.**

Every year, enormous sums of money get wasted by businesses that jump on the latest marketing bandwagon, or have knee-jerk reactions to perceived crises in customer enquiries. A Healthy Bouncy Business knows that the only strategy that will bring customers to its door consistently and profitably is one that relies on building relationships. And communicating at many levels and through many channels with its existing and prospective customers. Advertising in the Yellow Pages might have an impact, but only as part of an integrated business wide strategy. A Google AdWords campaign or Search Engine Optimisation will only work if the enquiries that come to your website result in effective and genuine communications between your company and the customer.

Marketing is not a department

The owner of a Healthy Bouncy Business realises that most activities of the business have an impact on marketing - and nearly all decisions that are taken in a business have a marketing dimension to them.

For example, a decision about the price charged for a business' services has a direct impact on the opportunities to do business, and as such is a marketing decision as well as a financial management decision. Increasing the price of a product can have the effect that the product will be perceived as a more desirable item; or it may also be that increasing the price simply leads to lower turnover. It can easily be demonstrated that a 'returns policy' can have a direct impact on marketing of the business: by having a 'no-questions asked' returns policy you communicate that you have absolute confidence in your product.

Here are some other examples of marketing:

- Answering the phone
- Sending an email
- If you build software: the error messages that pop up
- The after-dinner mint in a restaurant
- Warranty policies
- Quoting procedures
- Uniform policies
- Environmental sustainability policies

It is important to understand that every interaction between a business and its customers (or the external world at large) is an opportunity to market the business; to either positively or negatively affect its opportunities to do business.

Business owners of a Healthy Bouncy Business constantly ask themselves how its business processes impact its opportunities to do business.

The Brand Arrow... A brand is much more than a logo

- What do we do?
- What do we provide?
- What do they buy?
- How do they feel?

Brand

Josh's Bedtime Story

Once upon a time a long, long time ago in a land not unlike Australia... I worked with a small business owner called Josh, who had a successful air-conditioning contracting business. For many years Josh's business experienced wild swings: from having more work than he could handle, to scratching around to have enough to do for his teams. Whenever one of these lean periods would arrive, Josh would start to scramble for advertising or other marketing opportunities, generally with limited impact. And then, when the business was finally flowing in again, the whole concept of marketing would be forgotten until the next scary lean period.

One day I managed to convince Josh to engage a marketing consultant to develop a comprehensive marketing plan. The plan took many forms of marketing into account and took a long term view of the lead generation process. Josh started to implement the plan into his business consistently, week after week. After only six months he saw that the wild fluctuations had started to smooth out. A steady stream of high quality inquiries was coming to his doors.

And Josh lived happily ever after...

Next Steps

1. List all the points in your business at which your customers come in contact with you.
2. Ask yourself: What are the marketing opportunities at each of these points?
3. What could you do better at these points, from the customers' point of view?
4. Where are your customers, how can you talk to them, and why would they want to hear from you?
5. List five things you could do to make it easier for customers to do business with you.
6. List five new ways you could communicate with your customers.

Resources

- *The Ten Truths* Website: www.thetentruths.com.au/resources/marketing
- Article – Wendy Kenney, "Low Cost and No-Cost Marketing Tips": www.smh.com.au/small-business/growing/building-buzz-lowcost-and-nocost-marketing-tips-20101011-16et5.html
- Blog – Seth Godin: www.sethgodin.typepad.com
- Book – Barbara Findlay Schenck, "Small Business Marketing for Dummies" www.dummies.com/store/product/Small-Business-Marketing-For-Dummies-2nd-Edition.productCd-0471751030.html
- Book – Seth Godin, "Purple Cow", and many others www.sethgodin.com/purple/
- Video – Rory Sutherland on advertising and influencing perceptions: www.ted.com/talks/lang/eng/rory_sutherland_life_lessons_from_an_ad_man.html

Remember

Marketing evolves from the top down. It starts with the focus that you as the business owner display, and it must trickle down to every employee and every action of the business.

TRUTH 6

About Customers

Create Raving Fans

Who are they, where are they, what do they need?

It takes years to build a great reputation, and five minutes to lose it

A Healthy Bouncy Business gains a great deal of its ongoing and new business from word of mouth and referrals, which are all based on reputation.

Every successful business has satisfied customers, but referrals on the whole do not come from most satisfied customers. Only customers that have turned into fans or advocates of your business go out of their way to tell their family and friends about your business and their experience with it, and do so with such enthusiasm that actual business follows.

Satisfied customers will stick with a product or service until something better comes along. Sometimes satisfied customers will even disappear for no identifiable reason; simple boredom might be enough to lose these satisfied customers.

> **Customers who have been converted to fans, however, will actively resist other offerings because they feel personally and emotionally invested in the business. In turn, they feel that the business is truly committed to the relationship.**

Customers who have become fans of a business believe that the business truly cares for them, is interested in them, and takes full responsibility for managing the relationship between the business and the customer.

For customers to become advocates, or Raving Fans, of a business, they need to feel (at an emotional level, rather than a logical one) that:

- The business (and therefore its staff) acts with integrity and authenticity.
- The business has something truly useful to offer the customer.
- The business works to exceed the expectations of the customer, always.
- The relationship is about more than just money.
- The people in the business are passionate about the business.
- The business sees the customer as a partner in business.
- The business displays all of the above consistently.

Clearly the process of creating Raving Fans must start with creating satisfied customers, which is a challenging enough task in its own right. A Healthy Bouncy Business considers it to be the starting point, however, and will constantly be focused on the highest level of customer satisfaction. Ultimately, it is that last point, the consistency that often proves to hold the greatest challenge for most businesses.

Consistency is one of the greatest differentiators between a Healthy Bouncy Business and everyone else (also see final chapter, *Bonus Truth*).

The benefits of this consistent and constant focus on converting satisfied customers into enthusiastic advocates of your business are virtually immeasurable. The business owner who consistently creates Raving Fans will have only one significant problem - what to do with all the profit.

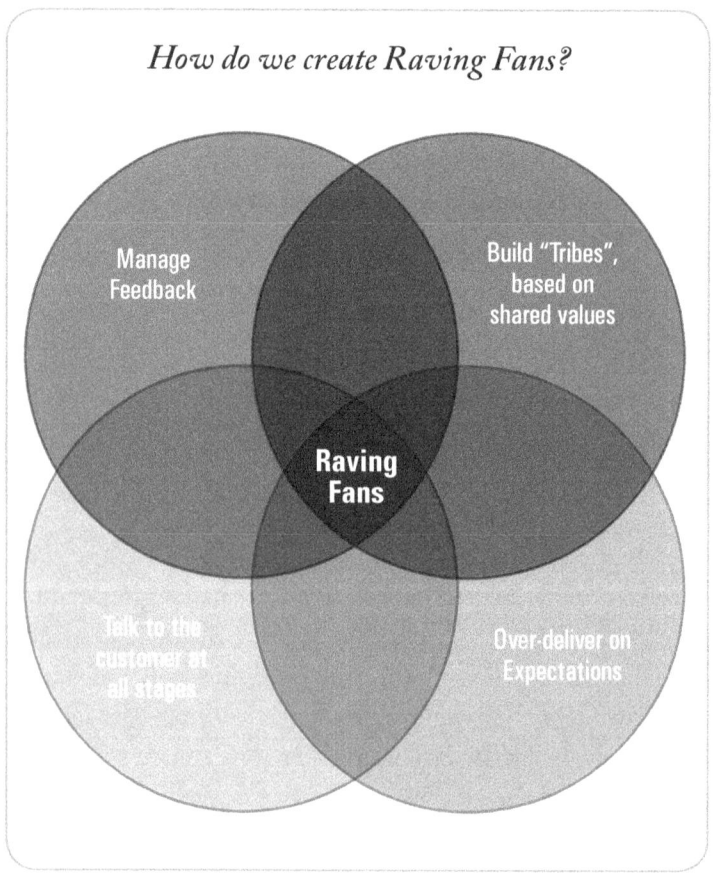

How do we create Raving Fans?

- Manage Feedback
- Build "Tribes", based on shared values
- Talk to the customer at all stages
- Over-deliver on Expectations
- Raving Fans

Daniel's Bedtime Story

Once upon a time a long, long time ago in a land not unlike Australia... I worked with a small business owner called Daniel, who owned a small supermarket in the inner city. For years Daniel's supermarket was travelling along ok with modest growth, enough to pay a reasonable wage to Daniel, but not much more. Customers would come and go, and if a new supermarket, deli or grocery store opened within a certain radius from Daniel's shop, he would lose a percentage of his customers for a while until he would slowly get back to where he was. Daniel's customers were usually quite satisfied - but nothing more.

When we started working together, we decided to focus on turning a significant percentage of Daniel's customers into Raving Fans. The process was a comprehensive one and included training his staff, putting on more specials, increasing his range and stock levels, raffles, a website, newsletters, and more. Though the essence of the process was that every week Daniel and I would ask this question: "What else would my customers want?"

Now a couple of years later, Daniel's turnover and profit have soared because his customers have become nearly evangelical in their support of his supermarket. Every week new customers turn up - because a friend has told them they simply must start shopping at Daniel's store. Daniel is about to repeat his winning formula in a second store in the city.

And Daniel lived happily ever after...

Next Steps

1. Ask yourself: What percentage of your customers are Raving Fans?
2. List your Raving Fan customers.
3. Write down the top five reasons why these customers are Raving Fans.
4. Create a list of ten or more customers who could be converted into Raving Fans.
5. What might be common strategies to convert these ten people into Raving Fans?
6. Pick the easiest strategy first and implement it. Today.

Resources

- *The Ten Truths* Website: www.thetentruths.com.au/resources/customers
- Book – Ken Blanchard, "The One Minute Manager Creates Raving Fans" www.blanchardlearning.com/templates/product.asp?product=10019
- Book – Michael Gerber, "The E-Myth Revisited" www.amazon.com/E-Myth-Revisited-Small-Businesses-About/dp/0887307280/ref=sr_1_1?s=books&ie=UTF8&qid=1286767103&sr=1-1
- Video – Ken Blanchard: Customer Service www.youtube.com/watch?v=YWlTADj6dF8&feature=related
- Video – Dr Dennis Rosen, "How to Loose a Customer": www.youtube.com/user/DrDennisRosen - p/u/1/Fk8uIGHCfiQ
- Video – Dr Dennis Rosen on how to stay in touch with your customer: www.youtube.com/user/DrDennisRosen - p/u/11/1PCaJODdDow

Remember

Customers do business with people - but only people they trust.

TRUTH 7

About Sales

Nothing happens until we sell something

How do we convert our 'stuff' into income?

People don't like to be sold to, but they love to buy

Selling can be one of the most rewarding aspects of the business operation. It is when we successfully make a sale that all the good work we have done in marketing, operations (see Truth 8), planning and product comes together. When someone buys our product or service, the message is: "You've done something right around here. So right in fact, that I am happy to pay money to get some of it."

Sales is also really hard. This part of a business can be confronting and challenging, and often it can be tempting to focus on many other aspects of a business while putting sales in the 'too hard basket'. Sometimes we get tempted to go with the fingers-crossed approach when it comes to sales. We hope that people will somehow find us, and be so keen to buy our product or service that we need to limit the number of people we let in the door at the same time. The sad reality is though, that unless you work for Apple, not many business people will live to have that experience.

If a business doesn't sell its products or services at a profit, it is a hobby - nothing more.

It is true that in this millennium people resist being 'sold to'. Much more so than they might have done 20 years ago. People want to buy from people they know and trust. Customers are more likely to buy from a business they believe cares about them. And customers love to deal with businesses that are passionately committed to their products and services. It is undoubtedly also true that you must ensure that customers are clear about the benefits they will get from your product or service and that they believe you will meet your promise to them.

At the same time, as business owners we can be forgiven for experiencing a 'no' to a sales offer as a personal rejection. Most of us are so personally invested in our business that we find it hard to make a distinction. Human beings will go to almost any length to avoid personal rejections. Our deep, unconscious brain actually experiences the fear of rejection at almost exactly the same level as the fear of death.

> **But nine times out of ten, if you do not at some point in the relationship ask for the business and make an actual offer to the customer with a 'call to action' that leads to a sale included in the offer, your business will not sell anything.**

But in most cases, unless you ask for the sale by making an actual offer to the customer (with a 'call to action' that leads to a purchase), your business will not sell anything. It is therefore the most uncomfortable of *The Ten Truths* that any owner of a Healthy Bouncy Business must come to terms with in his own way.

In order to create and sustain a Healthy Bouncy Business it is essential that:

- We must do sales.
- We must learn about sales.

- We must practice sales.
- We must develop and implement sales systems.
- We must learn to manage our fear of rejection.
- We must find ways to support ourselves to get up again when we have been rejected, so that we pick up the phone or knock on our prospects' doors once more.

A Healthy Bouncy Business makes sales, and sales are a constant focus in the business - in good times and bad.

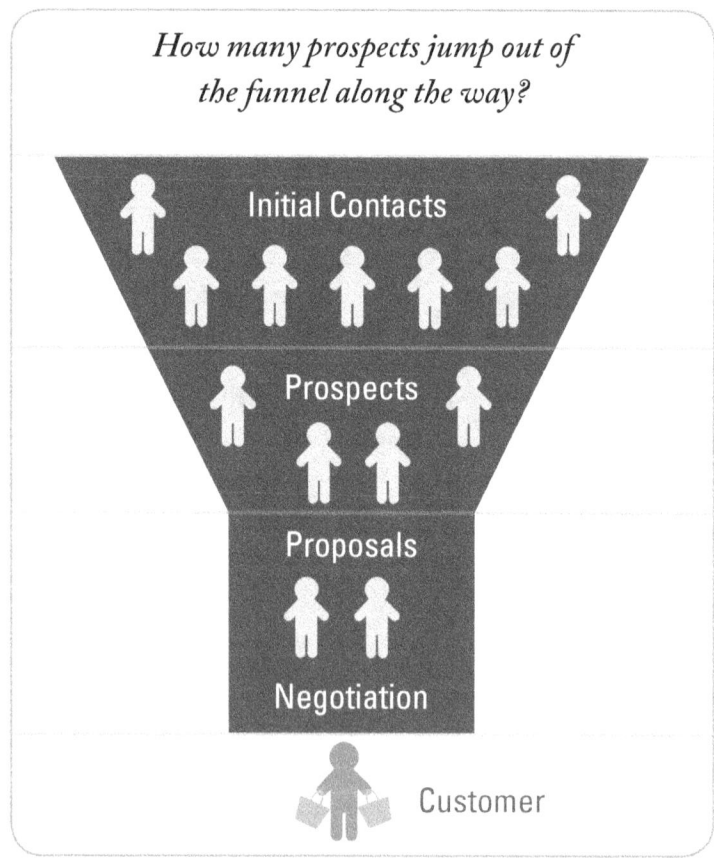

How many prospects jump out of the funnel along the way?

Kate's Bedtime Story

Once upon a time a long, long time ago in a land not unlike Australia... I worked with a small business owner called Kate, who owned an architectural practice. Kate was phenomenal at her profession and had won several prestigious architectural awards and prizes. Her portfolio was stunning, as were her website and brochures. All Kate's marketing materials shone with testimonials from Raving Fan clients. But when I started working with Kate she had barely enough work to keep the office going. The reason for this conflict was basic: Kate felt so uncomfortable selling herself and her business offer that she would go to enormous lengths to avoid asking for the sale. Only if clients specifically contacted her and asked her to take on their work did she bring business in.

Once we uncovered the issue, we started making headway with Kate's blocks and she learnt to become more comfortable with selling step by step. Kate's business has since gone from strength to strength.

And Kate lived happily ever after...

Next Steps

1. Accept that rejection is part of sales.
2. Accept that you will not sign up every opportunity.
3. Accept that rejection feels uncomfortable and that you will never learn to enjoy it.
4. Measure your sales performance.
5. Investigate sales training - online, or face-to-face.
6. Fill an A4 page with the following sentence, listing all the benefits, skills and knowledge you give your customers: "When people buy from me they get..."
7. List the top three benefits of buying your product or service.
8. List three things you could do to increase the level of trust your prospects and clients have in you.
9. Experiment with writing sales scripts, including an 'ask for the business' call to action.

Resources

- *The Ten Truths* Website: www.thetentruths.com.au/resources/sales
- Book – Jeffery Gittomer, "Little Red Book of Selling" on Amazon www.amazon.com/Little-Red-Book-Selling-Principles/dp/1885167601/ref=sr_1_1?s=books&ie=UTF8&qid=1286767145&sr=1-1
- Video – Jeffrey Gittomer on sales: www.youtube.com/user/BuyGitomer
- Video – Brian Tracey, "The Power of Asking": www.youtube.com/watch?v=At8FlN0kYiY&feature=related
- Video – The Black Chair, "The Love and Hate of Selling": www.youtube.com/watch?v=GV1Vjil155M
- Video – Alec Baldwin in 'Malice'. How not to do sales in 2011 and beyond: www.YouTube.com/watch?v=zCf46yHIzSo&feature=related

Remember

Helping people make the
right buying decision
is actually fun and
rewarding for both parties.

TRUTH 8

About Operations

Do more of what works, and less of what doesn't work

How do we best produce our 'stuff'?

Find the smallest difference that makes a difference

Operations is all about processes, systems and procedures. Whole libraries have been written on these topics, and many of the great universities in the world devote significant resources to this field in their MBA programs. Some of the big-name topics of the field are 'Continuous Improvement', 'Quality Assurance Systems', 'Just in Time', 'Six Sigma', 'Six Disciplines' and 'Lean Manufacturing'. There are whole sections of bookshops dedicated to doing business the 'McDonald's Way', the 'Toyota Way', the 'Jack Welch Way' or the 'Ryan Air Way'.

It is undeniably true that the principles of 'Continuous Improvement' and its many brethren are powerful. Implementing them properly and appropriately in any business can deliver a great return on investment.

In small businesses, however, we have limited scope to apply the methodologies in full. Often the cost of engaging specialist consultants to help with developing such systems can be prohibitive.

> **To create a Healthy Bouncy Business, we must therefore learn how to implement the essence of operations improvement ourselves to gain the benefits and stay ahead of the pack.**

The saying "do more of what works, and less of what doesn't work" reflects this essence. To be able to do more of what works and less of what doesn't, we have to investigate what actually does works and what does not. In order to do that we must measure our operations in our business.

For example, if we want to deliver more pizzas each day without increasing our delivery cost, we might measure the number of deliveries each delivery person makes per day and find out where the variances are. Once we know who delivers most pizzas per day, we can set out to discover what this person does different to the other drivers. We can then train the other drivers what to do to improve their delivery numbers.

The process must always start with measurement. Once the measurement has been carried out we can start to figure out what does and doesn't work, and begin to do more of what works - and less of what doesn't.

The continuous improvement cycle

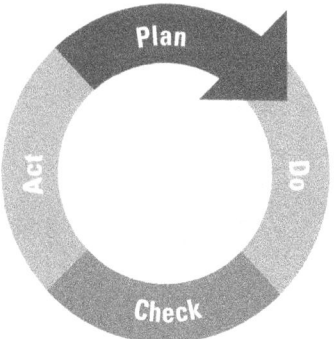

This is the famous Plan, Do, Check, Act Cycle *that Toyota, for example, used to become a number one in the world.*

Plan to do something, do it, check what worked. Then do more of what worked - and less of what didn't.

Matt's Bedtime Story

Once upon a time a long, long time ago in a land not unlike Australia... I worked with a small business owner called Matt, who owned a corporate video production company. A great deal of the work and cost in video production is incurred in cutting and editing, turning the raw footage from a number of cameras into one ten-minute video. Matt employed several editors and camera operators to do most of the work under his supervision.

A major source of frustration for Matt were cost and time over-runs. Some jobs would be delivered on time and with profit left for Matt, and some videos just wouldn't. Matt had looked at how he calculated his estimates. He had looked at production costs, his staff, types of clients, and projects - but nowhere could he identify anything that pointed at the problem.

When we started working together, this issue was giving Matt sleepless nights and he felt that running his business was like being dependent on the horse races for his financial security.

Given everything Matt had already looked at, I suggested we start from scratch. We decided to do some really basic measurement of the steps that were being taken in the process: from obtaining a brief from a client, through quoting and writing the scripts, to shooting and editing. Effectively, Matt stepped back and became the observer with a clipboard. He followed himself and his staff through all the operations and steps in the processes. For a whole week he made notes at ten minute intervals.

Suddenly, something started to become clear from his observations. The jobs that lost money had significantly less time spent on talking to the clients at the initial inquiry stage, quoting, writing the script and briefing the staff. In other words, the jobs that ran over time and over budget were rush-jobs. And because of the client's hurry, some of the standard checks and specifications would be passed over.

From that discovery it became obvious what needed to happen. Matt implemented a range of solutions to the problem, including raising his prices for rush-jobs and turning down some of those jobs. He identified which of the standard checks and specifications were critical in the process and could never be passed over. Six months later, Matt was sleeping well.

And Matt lived happily ever after...

Next Steps

1. List all the aspects of your business (marketing, operations, sales, customers, etc.).

2. List three main actions/tasks in each area (answering the phone, number of new leads followed up, responding to emails, sending out invoices, scheduling jobs, etc.).

3. Think of a way to measure the outcome of each of those operations.

4. Think of a way to improve the operation, using the measurements.

Resources

- *The Ten Truths* Website: www.thetentruths.com.au/resources/operations/
- Article - Roland Hanekroot: The world's greatest business tool revealed www.thetentruths.com.au/Downloads/Greatest-Business-tool.pdf
- Website - The Process Ninja: www.theprocessninja.com/
- Book – Michael Gerber, "The E-Myth revisited" on Amazon: www.amazon.com/E-Myth-Revisited-Small-Businesses-About/dp/0887307280/ref=sr_1_1?s=books&ie=UTF8&qid=1286767103&sr=1-1
- Book – Chip Heath and Dan Heath, "Switch, How to change when change is hard" www.heathbrothers.com/switch/

Remember

Measuring doesn't have to be really complicated, and it doesn't need to be scientifically perfect.

What matters is that you measure the differences between yesterday and today, the relative differences not the absolute ones

(see also Truth 3, About keeping your Finger on the Pulse).

TRUTH 9

About Staff

Attract the brightest, keep the brightest

How do we engage our people?

Your staff provide both your greatest challenges and your greatest rewards.

Businesses are about people. Without people a business can't exist. People are the owners, the staff, the families, the contractors, the suppliers and the customers.

To raise a Healthy Bouncy Business however, your staff must get extra special attention.

This process must start by making every effort to only hire people who will fit in, who have enthusiasm, energy and resourcefulness that is well above average. The old saying goes: "Hire for attitude and train for skill." In other words, finding staff with the right attitude is much more important than skill, because skill can be taught.

Once you have found the staff with the right attitude, you have to make sure you keep them. Staff turnover is one of the greatest hidden costs facing business. Recruitment and training - as well as the loss of efficiencies that come with bringing new people into a team - can often cost as much as 50% to 100% of a year's salary. It can also be shown that businesses with high staff turnover are not getting out of their staff what they might: it indicates that staff are not engaged and motivated in their work.

> **To attract the brightest and keep the brightest, requires a single-minded focus that rivals that of finding customers and generating business.**

The owner of a Healthy Bouncy Business is always focused on recruiting. Just like he might have a database and system for keeping track of clients and prospects, he has a system for keeping track of potential recruits. Just as the business owner might hold drinks in his office for his clients every few months to build solid relationships into the future, so he has drinks for his potential recruits to build the same long term relationships.

Attracting and keeping the brightest also involves creating a work environment that people want to work in. It requires having processes in place to select the brightest people from the many who might want to work for you. Attracting and keeping the brightest requires making it a priority to help your staff develop and grow. It means making it your mission to find out what makes your staff tick and how you can help them do their best work. It involves your learning to understand that people are motivated by many things besides money, and that people want to be part of something bigger than just making profit for the company.

A Healthy Bouncy Business does much more than pay lip service to these statements. There will be a constant focus on these principles at all levels of the business. As a result, people will line up to work for the business - making it possible for the business owner to actually engage the brightest.

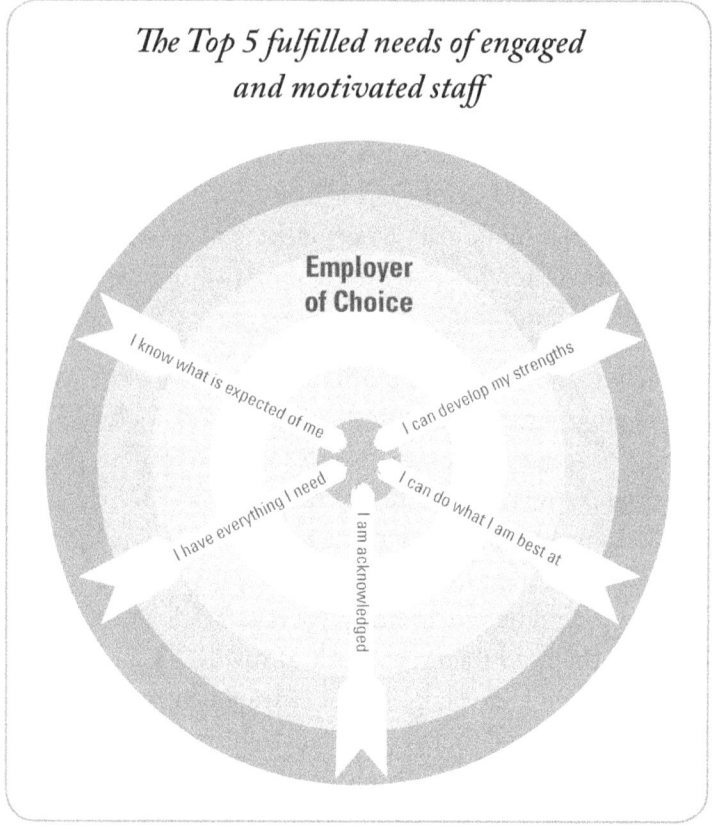

The Top 5 fulfilled needs of engaged and motivated staff

Tony's Bedtime Story

Once upon a time a long, long time ago in a land not unlike Australia... I worked with a small business owner called Tony, who owned an interior design business. Most of Tony's staff were designers of varying levels of seniority. Young designers especially tend to be highly itinerant, moving from company to company a great deal. Good designers are really hard to find. It certainly was Tony's experience that the good ones were not the ones replying to job ads: the good ones would rarely be out of work.

When we started working together Tony dreaded the request for a one-on-one meeting from his staff, because invariably this would be about announcing that the staff member was moving on to another company or overseas. We realised that this was simply going to be a feature of his industry for the foreseeable future. We decided that a strategy had to be devised to build a pipeline of good candidates, so that when someone resigned, Tony could simply pick up the phone and ring a few pre-qualified designers who would be keen to come and work for him.

We developed a plan and strategies. This included putting on four seminars about industry developments for young designers every year. It also required developing relationships with the local design schools. Then Tony created all sorts of social media strategies. And he made it known to his existing staff that they would get a significant financial bonus for introducing a new staff member.

Now, a few years later, Tony lets his staff go with his blessing. He regularly keeps in touch with all his ex-staff and several have indicated they would love to come back at some stage. There is a constant flow of exciting and enthusiastic young designers in and out of his business - and the practice is buzzing.

And Tony lived happily ever after...

Next Steps

1. Ask yourself: Would you want to work for your business? And long term?

2. What is the average time that staff stay? Is it more, or less, than one year?

3. Start building a database of prospective employees (just like the CRM system you use for clients).

4. List five places you could find the next star employee.

5. Begin the process of creating role descriptions for all jobs. A simple, bullet point form is sufficient.

Resources

- *The Ten Truths* Website: www.thetentruths.com.au/resources/staff/
- Article – Roland Hanekroot: "How to get and keep great staff 1 www.thetentruths.com.au/Downloads/Great-staff-1.pdf
- Article – Roland Hanekroot: "How to get and keep great staff 2 www.thetentruths.com.au/Downloads/Great-staff-2.pdf
- Book- Marcus Buckingham, "First Break all the Rules" gmj.gallup.com/content/1144/first-break-all-rules-book-center.aspx
- Book – Ken Blanchard et al: "The one Minute Manager" on Amazon www.amazon.com/One-Minute-Manager-Kenneth-Blanchard/dp/0688014291/ref=sr_1_1?s=books&ie=UTF8&qid=1286767232&sr=1-1
- Book - Ken Blanchard et al, "The one Minute Manager creates high performing Teams" on Amazon: www.amazon.com/Minute-Manager-Builds-Performing-Teams/dp/0061741205/ref=pd_sim_b_3

- Book – Steve Lunden, "Fish" on Amazon: www.amazon.com/Remarkable-Boost-Morale-Improve-Results/dp/0786866020/ref=sr_1_1?s=books&ie=UTF8&qid=1286767332&sr=1-1
- Worksheet/ Tool - Twelve questions for engaged staff survey (From Marcus Buckingham) www.thetentruths.com.au/Downloads/twelve-questions-staff-survey.pdf

Remember

Once our basic needs are met, money does very little (if anything) to motivate us.

It is a useful way to keep score, however.

TRUTH 10
About the Business Owner

Your time, health and brain cells are gold

How do we get what we need from our business?

Always remember: the business must work for you, not the other way round

Small business owners generally work more hours on average, every week, than employees. They do this because they are passionate about their business, because they are completely invested in their business, and because they often have a sense of "if I don't do this thing, no one else will". Also, there is an acceptance, almost an expectation, in our society that as a business owner you are meant to be the one who unlocks the door in the morning as well as the one who switches off the light at the end of the day.

It is also the case that many small business owners have started their business because they have the skill and experience. The owner might have been a particularly effective tradesperson or professional - such as an electrician or an architect -, and on the strength of that skill started the business.

It can easily be understood that with that kind of background there is an expectation that the success of the business is directly related to the number of hours the owner is involved in the 'work of the business'. He is often doing the actual electrical work or the actual architectural planning. Ultimately, the most profitable electrical work or the best architecture is going to be performed by the owner. Hence a lot of the actual work of the business owner - the managing, creating, visioning, building, controlling and planning -

becomes a secondary priority, and is undertaken at night or on the weekends. Or not at all.

> **To raise a Healthy Bouncy Business however, the business owner must learn that the most valuable resources of the business are his time, health and brain cells. They cannot be replaced.**

None of the other resources of the business (people, materials, equipment, machines and capital) are limited. You can buy, hire or borrow more of every one of them.

Once the owner comes to understand that his personal resources limit the business development, he will start to ask himself: is spending so many working hours doing the architectural or electrical work actually the best use of his very limited time? He will start to question whether working at night, day in day out, to do the vital work that no one else in the business can do is the best use of his very limited vitality. He will start to wonder whether the most crucial work of the business owner shouldn't better be carried out during the optimum work hours of the day (instead of late at night). All the while ensuring that his health is in an optimum state to make the most of this work.

To raise a Healthy Bouncy Business, the business owner must make 'the work of the business owner' his first priority and responsibility. When he learns to accept that responsibility, he will start to guard his health jealously and protect every minute of his day fiercely.

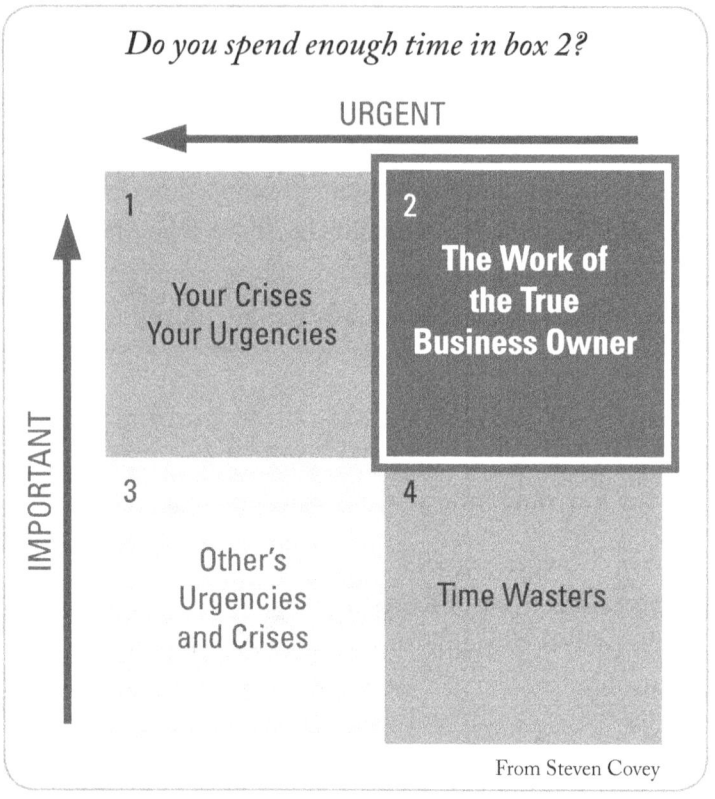

From Steven Covey

Megan's Bedtime Story

Once upon a time a long, long time ago in a land not unlike Australia... I worked with a small business owner called Mega, who sold promotional products. When I started working with Megan, her business had been stagnating for a couple of years. Every time a new client came on board another client fell off. Megan worked incredible hours and was starting to get a little frustrated. She was at risk of burning out.

Early in our work together I realised that her work hours

were simply unsustainable and we went through an exercise to see how she spent her time. I asked her to keep track of her day in 15-minute intervals for a week and enter that information into a spreadsheet. Megan found that she spent an enormous amount of time doing administration work to manage the orders and organise the import of items from China. Megan felt that she couldn't afford to employ someone to do that kind of work and that it was too risky to lose control over some of these jobs.

I asked her to reflect on the cost of not delegating these responsibilities, and on what other jobs tended to fall by the wayside because she did all this administration work. In the end, Megan came to the conclusion that her time was too valuable to do the paperwork or to look after the logistics of importing goods. We developed systems that allowed her to delegate those functions while keeping her finger on the pulse (see Truth 3).

With Megan freed up to do the real 'work of the business owner' rather than the 'work of the business', her business soon started to turn around. A couple of years later her business has doubled in turnover and improved its profitability significantly.

And Megan lived happily ever after...

Next Steps

1. List all the functions in your business that must be done by you as the business owner.

2. Which functions do you do now that are not the best use of your time?

3. Keep a pad with you for a day and write down everything you do in small intervals, as small as five minutes.

4. Transfer the items to a spreadsheet and group like with like (administration, marketing, client crises, employee issues, etc.).

5. List how much time you get in a day for the 'work of the business owner'.

Resources

- *The Ten Truths* Website: www.thetentruths.com.au/resources/you/
- Book - Stephen Covey, "The 7 Habits of Highly effective People" on Amazon: www.amazon.com/Habits-Highly-Effective-People/dp/0743269519/ref=sr_1_1?s=books&ie=UTF8&qid=1286767474&sr=1-1
- Article – Roland Hanekroot: "If you do what you usually do..." www.thetentruths.com.au/Downloads/The-Secret.pdf
- Article – Roland Hanekroot: "Hard work never made anyone Rich" www.thetentruths.com.au/Downloads/Hard-work.pdf
- Tool - Steven Covey's "4 Quadrants" time management tool www.thetentruths.com.au/Downloads/4quadrants.pdf

Remember

Being a great carpenter is a wonderful reason to start a carpentry business.

But to build a great carpentry business, you also need to make time and space to be a great manager and a great CEO.

BONUS TRUTH

About *The Small Business Bootcamp*™

Keep yourself accountable

How do we make it all happen?

Knowledge doesn't lead to success.. Action does

As I wrote in the introduction, we don't often come across new knowledge and I certainly don't expect that the great business gurus of this world like Ken Blanchard, Ram Charan, Michael Gerber and Tom Peters are going read *The Ten Truths* and slap themselves on the forehead, exclaiming: "Why didn't I think of that before!"

I once saw a stand-up comedy sketch where the comedian said: "I hope someone asks me to write a diet book one day; I know exactly how to write it and it would be the shortest book in history… Chapter one: Eat less… Chapter two: Are you eating less yet?"

Losing weight is not only about knowledge. Nor is creating sustainable businesses. The knowledge is important, and I believe that being aware of the significance of *The Ten Truths* is a great first step.

> **The next step, however, is taking action - and doing so consistently, day in day out, week in week out, year in year out. Every journey starts with the first step, but the only way to complete the journey is to take the next step, and the next step, and the next one.**

Consistency is the key; it is the one thing that makes it all come together in the end. Just as the only way to lose weight is to eat less today, tomorrow and the day after, i.e.

consistently, so you will only achieve your goals in business if you practice consistency.

Consistency is hard

Consistency is hard for everyone, but when you are the owner of a business you are all alone out there. No one will keep you accountable, no one will pull you into line and no one will reach out a hand to keep you steady when the floor under your feet starts to wobble every now and then.

For this reason I believe that the most important thing any small business owner can do to keep himself on track – to remain consistent, confident and focused -, is to put a support mechanism in place.

There are many ways to do this, depending on your circumstances and your needs. You can find a business coach or mentor, or you can put in place an Advisory Board of one or more people you have respect for.

I have created The *Small Business Bootcamp*™ to be a support mechanism for small business owners: www.smallbusinessbootcamp.com.au.

> **The Bootcamp is a six month intensive program for Small business owners who want to create Big Change in their business in a Short Time.**

It includes regular one-on-one sessions, monthly group coaching sessions and monthly group training sessions where you learn about *The Ten Truths*, learn how to implement them, and then actually put them in place step by step by step. The reason it is called the *Bootcamp* is because it is tough. It promises hard work, sweat and tears - but it also promises to be one of the most rewarding and exciting six months of your business life.

The *Small Business Bootcamp*™ is successful for many reasons, but one of the primary reasons is accountability. When you enrol in the *Bootcamp* you will have no choice but to be consistent, and your progress will be inevitable.

Not everyone who reads this book will be able to enrol in the *Small Business Bootcamp*™. I only run a face-to-face *Small Business Bootcamp*™ in Sydney, Australia, at this stage. And I only work with a very limited number of business owners at any one time, to be able to give them my full attention. Most of you will therefore need to find another way to keep yourself accountable and there are many good people and organisations out there for you. But make no mistake: when you start implementing *The Ten Truths* and keep yourself accountable to take the next step, and the next, and the next... every day, you *will* raise your own Healthy Bouncy Business.

Believe me, you too will live happily ever after...

If you have a great Ten Truths *story of your own, I'd love to hear about it.*

Send me an email to roland@thetentruths.com.au and I will include your story on the www.thetentruths.com.au website.

Next Steps

1. Find someone to keep you accountable.

Resources

- www.smallbusinessbootcamp.com.au
- www.linkedin.com/groupRegistration?gid=2770405
- A good place to find qualified coaches is via the ICF www.coachfederation.org/
- A great coach training organisation is Results Coaching systems: www.resultscoaches.com/
- There is a list of some great coaches on my website: newperspectives.com.au/Webresources.htm

Remember

The world is full of wonderful ideas and dreams.

Raising a Healthy Bouncy Business, however, is about doing stuff.

About the Author

I am Roland Hanekroot, owner and founder of *New Perspectives Business Coaching*, as well as *The Institute of Small Business Coaching*. I am accredited by the Institute as a Master of Small Business. I am also the *Small Business Bootcamp*™ trainer.

I came to business coaching, mentoring and consulting from a small to medium business background. I have some 20 years' experience as the founder and owner of several successful businesses in construction, IT and business consultancy.

I originally trained as a journalist in The Netherlands and worked for a national daily newspaper in Amsterdam. Later, I became a builder and project manager in the construction industry (residential) here in Australia. I have also worked and lived in Greece, the Caribbean, England, and Italy.

I am a certified coach with *Results Coaching Systems* and have carried out extensive further advanced coach training with *Results* and other organisations. I have studied in the areas of executive, business and team coaching, and specialised coaching tools and models.

Besides my coaching credentials I am a qualified volunteer telephone-counsellor with *Lifeline Sydney* and I am trained in NLP and Neuro Semantics, as well as Solution Focused Brief Coaching. I hold a Certificate IV in Workplace Training and Assessment (TAA), and I am a certified Small Business Counsellor (APEC). I use a variety of the tools from all these different disciplines, as appropriate, in my coaching work.

My background, skills and experience, as well as the ongoing training I have and will continue to undergo, place me in a unique position. I am able to combine my background and training as a small business owner and entrepreneur with my qualifications in coaching, training and related disciplines. In other words: I wear two hats. Which means I am able to offer my clients the best of both worlds, coaching and business mentoring.

I live in the inner city of Sydney, and operate *New Perspectives Business Coaching* out of my office in Elizabeth Bay. I also work with clients at their premises when appropriate, and because coaching can very effectively be done by telephone, my clients come from all over the world.

Are You Ready to Start to Make a Difference... ?

Roland Hanekroot
NEW PERSPECTIVES COACHING

www.ingramcontent.com/pod-product-compliance
Lightning Source LLC
Chambersburg PA
CBHW050600300426
44112CB00013B/2006